MW01098826

United We Came

A Personal Account from Ground Zero

BY MARY STEPHENS, R.N.

RED CROSS VOLUNTEER

LC LONGWOOD COMMUNICATIONS

This book or parts thereof may not be reproduced
in any form, stored in a retrieval system or transmitted
in any form by any means—electronic, mechanical, photocopy,
recording or otherwise—without prior written permission of the
publisher, except as provided by United States of America copyright law.

Copyright © 2002 by Mary Stephens, R.N.
All rights reserved
Library of Congress Catalog Card Number: 2002110424
International Standard Book Number: 1-883928-44-3

This book is not sponsored, endorsed
or authorized by the American Red Cross.

Published by:
Longwood Communications
3037 Clubview Drive
Orlando, FL. 32822
(407) 737-6006

Cover and interior design:
Geoffry Sprague/Quidoki Inc.

Typography: Lillian L. McAnally

Photography Credits
Cover: Ira Sapir
Back Cover: David Mieras/Mackinac Graphics LTD
Interior Photos (except as noted): Ira Sapir
Page 123: Mary M. Stephens
Page 127: Ginny Yost

To contact the author about speaking
to your church or organization:
marycstephens@cs.com
9885 Winegar Road
Redding, CA. 96003

Printed in the United States of America

02 03 04 05   🦅   7 6 5 4 3 2 1

DEDICATION

*In honor of those
who gave of themselves
and their resources
during the recovery effort
September 11, 2001.*

Acknowledgements

I would like to express my heartfelt thanks to the dedicated workers and volunteers who gave of their time and superhuman effort during the 9-11 recovery. To my friend and fellow nurse, Bert Speegle. I couldn't have gone through it without you. Also, to the countless others whose paths crossed mine at pier 94, you left indelible footprints upon my heart that will forever be with me wherever I go.

When mentioning volunteers, we visualize the people who physically go and do the hands-on work. I would like to say from experience that the family and friends supporting and encouraging the volunteers were more vital to their success than any other component. I personally could not have done it without all of you. Special friends like Russell Swartz, who called often, and was waiting at my home to surprise me with a fancy sit-down dinner complete with table flowers and candles. Friends and co-workers like Betty Watson, my Red Cross nursing assistant, always there to lend an helping hand, allowing me to leave knowing that my chapter was being cared for. My sister and brother-in-law, Margie and Dan Van Zant, and sister Rose Bowen, sisters-in-law Diane Wicker, Gloria Pearson, Sally Stephens; and cousin Glenda Sanders. They kept me uplifted with phone calls and cards and most importantly prayers.

A special thanks to the folks at Longwood Communications: Murray

Fisher, Lillian McAnally, Stephanie Reeves and Geoff Sprague for their great work. And to my special research assistant, Bufford G. Deale.

And finally the biggest thank you to my best friend and husband for supporting my dreams and doing everything he can to make them possible. You are truly an outstanding

Ira Sapir, who was injured during his time helping look for survivors, was one of approximately 6,500 volunteers in the first six months after 9-11.

volunteer.

A special thanks to Ira Sapir, a young man who answered the call of his heart to help and received a debilitating shoulder injury in the process. Many of the pictures I share with you were taken by him.

United We Came

Foreword

My journey did not begin on 9-11. It began as a small child hearing stories about starving children in Africa. I can't count the times I was told to eat my food because there were hungry kids that would love to have it. Does that sound familiar? I could not understand why my mother didn't just send the turnip greens and boiled okra directly to Africa if it was needed so badly. After all, I was more than willing to sacrifice my share.

While learning to read and write I would sit seemingly for hours creating stories of how I would grow up to become a missionary nurse and save those hungry, sick children. I had aspirations of being like the modern-day Mother Teresa, even before I knew there was such a person.

Although I grew up with idealistic dreams of saving the world, the realities of adulthood have a way of punctuating our lives with many twists and turns.

In December of 1966 I married my high-school sweetheart and my life as a new wife temporarily replaced all other lofty ambitions. Roy was my "knight in shining armor" and my primary focus was now on him. I dearly loved him and developing our relationship took precedence over everything else.

Eventually we had two children of our own and motherhood was far more important to me than childhood dreams. Like a family heirloom that is occasionally held, carefully dusted and then returned to its appointed place, my dreams would only come to mind during occasions of wishful thinking and what ifs. In those special moments I would let them dance freely in my mind and then put them gently away knowing that their fulfillment may never be.

The realities of adulthood have a way of punctuating our lives with many twists and turns.

Soon after our two sons entered college, the restlessness of unfulfilled dreams started creeping in more often. Knowing how much I wanted to be a nurse, Roy would ask "Why don't you go to college and become an R.N.?"

At first I made excuses like "I'm too old" and "my grades in high school were not good enough," but Roy didn't give up that easily. In reality I didn't have confidence in myself. But he kept saying, "You can do it!" So, with his encouragement, much soul searching, fear and prayer, I started college at the age of 38. For the next four years my family generally saw the back of my head because my face was in a study book.

With their patience, ongoing support and the help of fellow students, I graduated as a registered nurse at the age of 42. At this point one very big part of my dreams was fulfilled and I could hardly believe it was true. Although I still hadn't become a Mother Teresa or helped the sick children in Africa, it was a start.

After practicing my nursing skills for five years in the local area, I was impressed with the need to volunteer my skills for the benefit of those who could not afford them. Both Roy and I felt the importance of giving something back to the country that had been so good to us. So, that conviction, coupled with my own personal desire to volunteer, eventually led me to join the American Red Cross. The following stories give you a brief overview of some of the events taken from a continuing journey that began with that organization in the summer of 1996.

UNITED WE CAME

9.11.01

I was sitting in the dining room enjoying my morning cup of hot herbal tea as my gray cat softly brushed against my feet. The morning sunshine was streaming in through my French doors and I was preparing for another normal day. Life was good, what more could I ask for?

One more day and we would be traveling to visit our youngest son, Randy, in Loma Linda, Calif. We would be meeting his new fiancée for the first time and spending a few days getting to know her. Then in two weeks Roy and I would be flying to the New England states to spend two glorious weeks looking at the vibrant colors of the fall. Yes, life was good and the excitement level was high.

The phone rang, and as expected it was my morning call from my sister Margie. Sometimes I would call her, other times she would call me. We usually each made a hot drink then talked a long time about a little of nothing, sometimes a little of everything. Today I assumed it would be no different when she called, but instead of a cheery "good morning," she quickly told me to turn on my television. She said a plane had hit the World Trade Center and the news coverage was showing the scene.

I quickly reached for the control knob and turned our television on. I called out to Roy who had not yet left for work, and together we watched the unfolding events for several hours. We were shocked that our country was being cruelly attacked. The thought that America, the country that usually protects others, would need protection herself sent chills down my spine. Could this really be happening? Was this a mistake? It looked so much like a Hollywood doomsday movie. With a heavy heart and tears streaming down my face, I prayed for the safety of the people in the buildings, then turned to Roy saying, "Honey, I have to go help them. I have to go."

I immediately called my supervisor at the local Red Cross Chapter where I am Disaster Health Services supervisor, informing them that I was willing and able to go at a moment's notice. My bags were packed and sitting by the door. At this point it was not a question of if but when.

The thought that America, the country that usually protects others, would need protection herself sent chills down my spine.

Since volunteering with the American Red Cross six years before, I have dealt with community losses, such as wildfires, residential fires and forest fires. In 1999 alone our Northern California area was hit with three major fires within a period of four months. Over 400 homes had been lost and one volunteer fire fighter had lost her life. In preparation for being summoned at a moment's notice, I always keep my overnight bag packed with essentials and my Red Cross I.D. Now the call I listened for would come from a much bigger scene.

Couldn't they see time was wasting? There were people hurting and I felt they needed me.

Knowing that the call could come in days or weeks, we decided to go ahead with our trip to Loma Linda. We knew that I could fly out from there just as well, so putting off that trip wasn't necessary.

I waited impatiently. A day passed, two days, three days and still no call. *Why*, I thought? We were willing to cancel our New England vacation plans and I had taken the appropriate training. Hadn't I responded to many disasters showing that I was capable? All these questions and more kept crossing my mind as we continued to follow the recovery efforts on the news.

United We Came

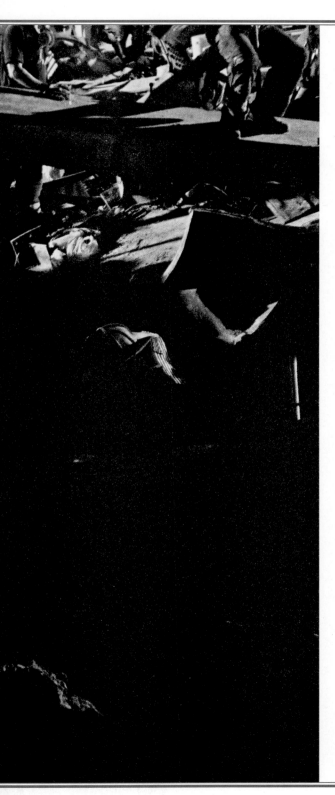

After we returned from our trip to Loma Linda, the call finally came. Vance Montgomery, my supervisor, asked to meet with me to go over some questions that needed to be answered before I could be seriously considered as a candidate for the recovery effort. Couldn't they see time was wasting? There were people hurting and I felt they needed me. Patience has never been a virtue of mine. As a little girl I was always jumping ahead of myself and getting into trouble. I could have avoided many missteps if only I had waited just a little longer for things to work out. Unfortunately I never out grew this and even now I find myself in various predicaments due to this character flaw.

The emotional and physical toll on all the Ground Zero workers was very heavy and long-lasting.

Some of the questions Vance asked were about my health. What kind, if any, medications was I taking? Had I had any family or close friends die in the last year? Could I work under hardship conditions and was I able to work long hours? I must have answered these to their satisfaction because two days later I was told that my name was going to be on the list of Red Cross nurses being sent on October 2nd, the second wave. October 2nd! I had to wait two more weeks. I was very impatient. I wanted to go now!

Being the first Redding Red Cross volunteer worker to go to a national disaster in 10 years generated a lot of local media attention. I was asked to do interviews on television and several radio stations. Our newspaper also had me go by their office for an interview. They wanted to write an article featuring me as I was preparing to leave and go to New York City. Once the word spread, everywhere I went people would come up to me and wish me well. My local church, as well as others, prayed for me. With all the support, I felt as if I was leaving with my emotional plate filled to overflowing. I knew I could handle anything that could come my way. After all, I was a nurse. I had dealt with sorrow and death before, so this couldn't be too much different. Besides, I had my family and friends' support, so what more could I need?

Day 1

As we waited at the airport for my departure, two local television reporters filmed my family and me for a segment to be aired on the evening news. After the interview, another passenger waiting for the same plane told me that his cousin had perished in the Twin Towers on 9-11.

We talked about the incident for a few moments and I had my first taste of what I had in store for me in the coming weeks. It brought tears to my eyes, but my confident and willing spirit had me fooled into believing I could handle whatever came my way.

After an emotional goodbye I boarded the plane to San Francisco, and as it lifted off I knew it would be three weeks before I saw those familiar faces again. My thoughts and feelings experienced wild gyrations from apprehensive to excited to tearful to all points in between. I really did not know how I should feel. All things considered, I would say that, for the most part, the first leg of my trip was a somber one. There was one bright point however that demonstrated the "spirit of America." A young man in his early 30's leaned forward in his seat and reached his hand out to give me something. As I took a closer look I realized that he was holding a twenty-dollar bill.

"Please take this and help someone when you get to New York," he said to me. "I wish I could give more, but this is all I can give. I haven't worked in a couple of months." He had witnessed my interview with the television reporters and wanted to do something to help. I thanked him but had to refuse the money. I explained that all donations had to be handled according to Red Cross guidelines and at this time I was not authorized to accept them. In further conversation I learned that he was a merchant marine and it was evident that he felt the need to reach out in any way he could.

The flight departing from San Francisco to New York was not even half full. I knew people were afraid to fly and I had my own concerns. As I looked around, only a few appeared to be visiting while the rest sat quietly, read or slept. My thoughts were unusually

My thoughts were unusually introspective as I reassured myself that I was a professional nurse and I knew I could handle anything that came my way.

introspective as I reassured myself that I was a professional nurse and I knew I could handle anything that came my way. My Red Cross supervisors had warned that this would be a difficult job but, "I'll show them how tough I am," was my response.

After arriving at JFK Airport at 10 p.m., I followed the written instructions given to me before leaving Redding. They included the after-hours phone number of Red Cross headquarters in New York, the name and address of my hotel and contact information for receiving job assignments. Although I had been traveling all day, I could hardly wait for the

... what greeted me on this trip was an eerie cloud of solemnness.

few hours to pass until I would find out what my assignment would be. As I mentioned earlier, patience is not one of my virtues. I set my clock, asked the hotel night manager for a 5:30 wake-up call for backup and then went to bed. I soon realized that it was a waste of time, for I spent the next few hours tossing and turning with little or no rest.

I had visited New York City twice before and remembered it as large, noisy and exciting. One would normally see small groups of people gathered in animated conversation and many others simply sightseeing or shopping. Add to this mix the fast-paced walk of New York workers

UNITED WE CAME

rushing to and from places of employment, the sounds of automobile horns, emergency sirens and squealing tires. These sights and sounds probably give an accurate description of any great city in the world. Unlike the past, what greeted me on this trip was an eerie cloud of solemnness. There was little if any horn blowing, only a few people openly conversed and non-verbal communication seemed more cordial. I noticed people uncharacteristically willing to go the extra mile with politeness and drivers demonstrating less hostility toward one another. The whole city appeared to be in mourning. I saw an office building five stories tall wrapped in

All over the country, businesses and individuals showed their patriotism and support of America by displaying the flag on buildings, cars and houses.

a large American flag. It was honorably draped and instantly reminded me of a shroud covering a coffin. As I walked about, most of the buildings displayed our country's flag in one form or another. Some were hanging from flagpoles, some were hanging from windows and still others were displayed inside in prominent places to show unity. As I blinked the tears from my eyes, I knew that I was seeing the heart and soul of New York City demonstrating their love, their sorrow and their pride in the best way they could. I saw a unified city assuring the rest of this country that they, our brothers and sisters, would not bow to the terrorists.

As I viewed the landscape around me, suddenly I missed the snow-capped mountains that I was used to seeing at home in the northwest. I stared at the tall buildings reaching toward the sky and accepted the fact that these would have to be my mountains for the next three weeks.

Day 2

After a restless night, I dressed and made my way down to the hotel lobby at 6:30 a.m. I and other volunteers were told to meet there at this time in order to board a shuttle to Red Cross headquarters. Upon arrival at head-quarters we were instructed on policies and procedures for this attack. We were then informed that the attack perimeter would be handled as a crime scene rather than a disaster.

The new recruits were verbally instructed, then handed printed material emphasizing the need for regular contact with our family and loved ones back home. The need for absolute confidentiality was stressed and a list of contact phone numbers for leadership assistance was provided. I was also told that many would need mental health counseling and debriefing at the end of this assignment. I chuckled to myself for, as a trained nurse, I thought others might need this, but not me. I was just fine and was here to help others.

After being sent to the required

departments, I was advised of the new challenges facing the Red Cross. This attack was being handled somewhat differently than other disasters, and I was asked to sit in a waiting area with approximately 20 new arrivals. As we waited impatiently we exchanged names and home states in order to pass time. After approximately 30 minutes our supervisors began handing out the assignments and informed us that our name tag color would indicate the security level of our job. A yellow nametag with picture ID indicated access was limited to areas of service with no Ground Zero clearance. A green plastic tag with picture ID indicated complete access to all areas of the disaster. Since this was my first out-of-state assignment, I expected to be given an easy job with limited access. Previously, my experience was limited to dealing with forest fires that required the opening of overnight shelters in our local community. I had the responsibility of caring for clients that were forced to evacuate and then only in small numbers. In addition I had experienced evacuation myself in October of 1999 and in so doing had developed greater empathy for disaster victims.

Among the job assignments being issued to nurses in this attack were those of staffing first-aid clinics in a central supply warehouse, assisting in client service centers, participating in home outreach teams and manning respite centers. The outreach teams would visit clients in their homes when their ability to travel to established centers was limited. The respite centers were set up in large white tents at Ground Zero where volunteers would render first aid directly to the workers. Their services ranged from treatment of cuts, abrasions, physical exhaustion, smoke inhalation and other minor injuries to the handing out of breathing masks, warm smiles and encouraging hugs. As I anxiously waited I soon found out that my assignment would not fit the description of those listed above. In just moments several of us would be given a very unique assignment, one that would impact our lives forever.

As our names were called we were directed into two groups. One group received green ID tags and the other received yellow. When my turn came, I was surprised to receive a green tag indicating "Full Access." As I accepted my tag I immediately felt tension knots forming in my stomach. I wondered, *Will I be able to handle this?* Suddenly the overwhelming confidence I had felt before melted away with no prior warning.

Immediately following the September 11th attack, Mayor Guiliani sought a method to protect disaster victims from the prying eyes of the media and curiosity seekers. His solution was to be implemented in a building called Pier 94. Approximately the size of four football fields and bordering the Hudson River, Pier 94 was normally rented out for events

As I accepted my tag I immediately felt tension knots forming in my stomach.

that anticipated the attendance of large crowds of people. In the mayor's plan the building was used to house all the immediate services disaster victim's families would need. These services included the FBI, Police, Fire Departments, Social Security, DNA testing, Legal Services, FEMA, Salvation Army, the Crimes Victims Board of the State of New York, Red Cross and many others. The building and adjacent area was considered high security with absolutely no personal cameras or news photographers allowed. If caught with any camera or recording device, the perpetrator would be immediately arrested, removed from the premises and not allowed to return. Red Cross workers were warned that violators within their ranks would be stripped of their right to work for the organization for life.

The security of Pier 94 reminded me of a mother bear protecting her cubs with her own life. For the next three weeks I would be a part of this protective environment, and I was both apprehensive and honored.

After receiving our assignment, three other nurses and I boarded a bus that would eventually drop us off at Pier 94. Other Red Cross workers were also on this trip, and as we traveled to our destination, the overwhelming silence was coupled with feelings of unbelief as we observed the changes that September 11th had wrought.

People were walking as if in a daze and I noticed several large dump trucks loaded with debris from the WTC passing. A flag was flying from one of them as they passed like a funeral procession, respectfully transporting the remains of what had

been two of the most magnificent buildings in the world. The walls at the street corners were covered with yellow ribbons. Handmade posters were propped up on the curbs, garbage cans or anything that would support the weight of the cardboard. Words of hope were written everywhere during a time when miracles

With tension knots in my stomach, I wondered if I would be able to handle this. I was so tense that I hadn't noticed that my last name was misspelled.

were needed and hope clung to the slim possibility that survivors would be found. But for me it wasn't the sights or sounds that were the most threatening, it was the odor that was seeping around the closed windows of our air-conditioned bus. The smell of death and destruction was reaching my nose for the first time, and my confidence was slipping. The knots I had noticed earlier were now making my stomach hurt.

My uneasiness continued as we arrived at Pier 94. Looking out of the window, the first thing I saw was a large number of armed policemen standing guard at the entrance. The road in front of the Pier was a multilane road leading around the Island of Manhattan with access to all ports. But now, barricades with armed guards were blocking the entrance of this large building. Only authorized vehicles were allowed to proceed after a thorough inspection of all accessible compartments and a mirrored look at the undercarriage. In front of the building was a wall covered with the pictures of missing loved ones. Attached to the pictures were notes and phone numbers asking for any information on their whereabouts.

Our bus was stopped temporarily for inspection and then proceeded to a designated parking space.

Upon exiting the bus and before entering the building, we were required to pass through four

As I stood quietly looking at these brightly colored flags and mementos of love, I felt a deep sense of pride.

checkpoints, each having a minimum of two and sometimes four policemen. At the first checkpoint we were required to show our special ID tag, have our bags and purses inspected carefully and then move on to the next. The last three checkpoints required proof of ID, but not bag inspections. Once inside we saw a crowd of grieving, listless people accompanied by their family support group. Just inside the front door stood an armed military man cradling his well-polished assault rifle. We then went to a table just inside the entrance door and signed the registration book. Our names were printed in advance in a daily logbook and had to match our ID tag in order to pass the last security check.

Immediately upon entering the building, one of the first things that we noticed was wall-to-wall carpet in sections of red, white and blue. As I looked upward, numerous large American flags were hanging from the ceiling. The interior was sectioned off with movable office dividers covered in blue and white fabric. In addition, all stationary walls had pictures, letters and posters attached that had been received from all over the world. As I stood quietly looking at these brightly colored flags and mementos of love, I felt a deep sense of pride. After a few moments of gazing we were introduced to the Red Cross nurses that we were here to replace. The next event was a grand tour conducted by a nurse supervisor.

How does one adequately describe four acres of metal building housing such grief and sadness? People of all sizes, shapes and ethnicity were walking around with looks on their faces that reminded me of scenes from horror movies.

As we were taking our tour we were shown an area assigned to interpreters, others for the various governmental agencies, still others for ancillary services and finally the rest room facilities. A very special place called "the walk of bears" was located along a side wall approximately 100 feet from the designated entrance for families and victims. It is a long walkway that is cordoned off with a white chain that gives the effect of walking down a narrow aisle. Its adjoining wall is covered from top to bottom with photos and letters of those missing. Many had phone numbers to call if anyone had information on their condition or location. As I gazed intently my eyes began tearing and I found I could not focus on the writings. Below these photos and letters lovingly sat hundreds of teddy bears sent from survivors of the Oklahoma City bombing. Each bear had a special handwritten note that could only be read by World Trade Center surviving families. We were given explicit instructions that we could look at but not touch these bears.

As I pondered the wall covered in pictures and loving messages, my chest tightened as tears softly streamed down my face. I hadn't heard about any of this in the news. These were pictures of healthy, happy, beautiful people. Pictures of someone's wife, sister, daughter, husband or son. People who were actively living life one moment and the next minute their fate forever sealed in a pile of dust and rubble. I wondered which of the families here today were connected to the smiling faces staring back at me from this hallowed wall. My emotional plate was beginning to empty and I had to move on. My eyes would turn away, but my mind would never forget.

Walking on I noticed that one of the families had posted their daughter's picture on the far side of the ladies rest room. It was taped at almost eye level and hung alone on the stark white wall. I looked at her picture and felt another emotional lump in my throat. Would she be found? I would be seeing her smiling face each day as I walked to the ladies room.

As I pondered the wall covered in pictures and loving messages, my chest tightened as tears softly streamed down my face.

Would her family ever see her alive again? Her face would also be imprinted in my mind forever. I looked at all these pictures wondering, *Would anyone be found?* The likelihood of surviving three weeks under the steel and concrete was highly unlikely.

My tour of the facility continued as our guide showed us the area where the families would silently sit waiting for their turn to board a ferry to Ground Zero. Accompanied by mental health workers or spiritual leaders, these grieving, heartbroken people would be transported privately to view a 16-acre piece of land that tightly clung to either the bodies or lives of their loved ones. A place where their future was transformed forever, but on this day a place where they continued to grasp their last remnants of hope.

There were over 80 countries represented at Pier 94. Many traveled from their home countries for the specific purpose of bringing samples of the victims' DNA. Upon receipt, the sample would be carefully marked and later tested by the most modern equipment science has to offer.

For those seeking spiritual support there were private, homemade chapels. There were also partitioned areas for Jewish, Catholic, Protestant and Islamic faiths. Inside, each contained appropriate decor and other objects pertinent to the particular faith. Among other things, I noticed a rosary in the Catholic section, candelabras in the Jewish section, a prayer rug in the Eastern Religion section. Further inside I saw notable books specific to the faiths represented, and still others dealing with loss and grief.

As we continued walking, with heads turning this way and that, we found it difficult to take in all that we were seeing and hearing. We were taken to an area approximately 60 feet by 60 feet where paid workers and volunteers could go to eat and rest. Along the left wall stood a row of tables stacked buffet style with hot, freshly cooked food, candy bars, chips, cookies, fruit and a large double-door refrigeration

Rescuers worked around the clock taking enough time only to grab a bite to eat and catch an hour or two of sleep. Clean up consumed 262 days.

MARY STEPHENS, R.N.

unit that contained a variety of cold drinks. The center of the room was filled with tables and chairs to be used while eating, and the right side of the room had numerous recliners and couches for exhausted workers.

My attention was drawn to the area on the right where many exhausted firemen and policemen were resting. Most were sleeping through the noises created by the people in this large building. Even with several nearby televisions blaring, these exhausted, brave men seemed oblivious to anything around them. I was told that they were virtually working around the clock. They only took time to grab a bite to eat, catch an hour or two of sleep and then go back to the rubble in their ongoing effort to find a brother, father or friend. I turned to my new friend Bert and gave her a look that said, *What have I gotten myself into?*

At the end of the grand tour, we returned to our first-aid station to receive our instructions on what we, as Red Cross nurses, would be responsible for. We had tables set up with over-the-counter medications, such as cough drops, aspirin, salves, eye drops, bandages and various items that we might need. I learned that many of

I turned to my friend and gave her a look that said, "What have I gotten myself in to?"

our nation's companies donated hordes of supplies for their part in this recovery effort. A half dozen chairs were set at our aid station for blood pressure checks, exams and other forms of medical assistance. Since by this time our shift was almost over, the four of us newly assigned nurses were sent back to our hotels to get some much-needed rest. Thursday, October 4th, would be our first full day at work and today's tour should have clued us on things to come. First of all, our organization really cares about their volunteers. Second, we would be working long, hard, exhausting days under emotionally draining conditions. It was obvious from the start that my strong spiritual beliefs would be tested.

United We Came

Day 3

My new friends Bert, a registered nurse, Vennie, a mental health worker, and I decided to walk approximately 12 blocks to our job site. This brisk 30-minute walk gave us a chance to get better acquainted and form a friendship-support group. Along the way we commented on the quietness of this usually noisy city and read the patriotic posters in the storefront windows. We especially liked the ones that read "These Colors don't run."

As we crossed the well-guarded street in front of Pier 94, we reached in our purses, pulled out our ID tags, hung them around our necks and moved on to the first checkpoint. In orientation the previous day, we had been instructed that anything marked or otherwise indicating a connection with the Red Cross could not be worn in public. They reasoned that this city was faced with enough daily reminders of their loss and any unnecessary display of Red Cross paraphernalia would only deepen the depressed mood. After passing inspection and cheerfully greeting the outside security officers,

UNITED WE CAME

we entered the building, signed the daily register and received a pre-printed colored paper tag. Each tag indicated "volunteer" or "family member" in bold print and was issued by the Mayor's Office of Emergency Services. For security reasons, tag colors changed daily, and each had the date handwritten on it by security personnel. We detached the protective covering, stuck the tags to our clothing and began our assigned duties.

Bert and I seemed to hit it off right away. She was like an older sister, and having worked on a previous national disaster, was more than willing to mentor me. After morning greetings with other workers, Bert and I decided to take the aid carts and do rounds.

Smoke continued to rise from the rubble as rescue workers pressed on. Despite the use of respirators and masks, lung illness became a major threat.

Doing rounds meant pushing a portable first-aid station on wheels among the workstations set up inside this large building. Each workstation provided a specific service and clients would arrive, sign in and then wait in line for their turn. Sometimes the waiting time extended for hours and anyone leaving the line for any reason risked losing their place. Because of the high number of people seeking assistance, a loss of place in line could require the client to return another day to be processed. In order to assist those waiting, our nursing cart carried snacks, water and fruit juices in addition to medical supplies. During our round we passed these items out in large quantity. We also distributed large numbers of over-the-counter medications for

The rescue workers assisted as 108,144 truckloads were slowly being removed.

MARY STEPHENS, R.N.

headaches, stomach disorders and various other maladies.

During the morning an FBI agent came to our first-aid station to have his eyes washed. He had been working at the disaster site and constant contact with smoke was causing them pain and irritation. My help seemed such a small act of kindness, yet he thanked me profusely. Later I noticed a stately priest with thick silver hair walking slowly by. As he greeted us I observed the haggard look on his face, and the slumped posture. As nurses, we are trained to assess our patients both mentally and physically so I immediately felt that something was not right with this man. In order to evaluate further, I went up to him and introduced myself. We exchanged names and he shared that he had been at Ground Zero for the first nine days and nights. I asked if I could take his blood pressure and he gladly consented. He then came over and sat in one of the exam chairs located at our first-aid station. I pulled up his right sleeve, placed a blood pressure cuff around his arm and carried on a conversation as I assessed his answers.

He looked harried and exhausted, and when I read the blood pressure, I wasn't surprised to see that it was extremely high. During further conversation I discovered that he wasn't resting, eating or sleeping properly. Having noticed early on that dehydration and poor nutrition were common problems among the people here, I armed myself with a bottle of water and some healthy snacks and gave them to him. I also gave verbal nursing orders and ended with a little phrase that I would use often from that moment on, "I need a hug, would you mind?" I knew that hugs have healing properties and they show that you care and are willing to give of yourself to others. In reality I felt that he was the one that needed some form of tactile reassurance. He leaned over, gave me my hug, and promised to return in two hours for a recheck of his blood pressure. From that day on, when I was there, this caring man would stop by and let me give him a hug, and he in turn gave me word of encouragement and blessing. In retrospect I believe we both were blessed.

Pier 94 was a place where grief and comfort shared common space.

Another memorable figure that I met was a young Italian policeman stationed here. From day one he made it his job to stop by our first-aid station every day to check on us. He was tall, slim, had shiny black hair, and was always smiling and chewing gum. "Good day ladies," he would say, "is there anything I can do for you today? Is everything all right?" On each of my 21 days on this job I could count on his cheery greeting. Another officer would also come by daily asking if we had a spare cigarette. Each time we would laughingly respond with virtually the same answer, "No, you know that we don't smoke, and you know that you should quit." He would smile, salute us and wish us a good day, then walk on. We knew that was their way of caring for and protecting us, and we looked forward to their daily visits.

Pier 94 was a place where grief and comfort shared common space. Some dogs that were used at Ground Zero were regularly brought here after exhausting days of searching for survivors or remains. After long periods sensing the smell of death, these loyal animals would experience depression similar to that of humans. They would become listless, have difficulty eating and sleeping and need emotional comfort. Few can refuse to pet or hug a sad animal, so these dogs were brought to the family assistance center to receive comfort and rest. In addition, those doing the hugging and petting received needed emotional support to cope with their own grief and depression. There were dogs of every breed, size and color. Some of these animals wore little caps on their heads and some wore patriotic kerchiefs around their necks. One comfort dog was a rather large white poodle that most every one wanted to touch. It was freshly groomed and its soft white fur fluffing out reminded me of the "big hair" styles seen in the sixties. This dog was very well behaved and did tricks upon command. Another dog, a German Shepherd, reminded me of my own special German Shepherd at home. Hugging him restored a few needed morsels to my own emotional plate.

Some time later, Bert and I were

The precarious position of the standing debris was a constant threat to the safety of the rescue workers. Some sustained injuries on the job.

MARY STEPHENS, R.N.

again making rounds with the aid cart, passing out more headache medications and refreshments. As we passed, a middle aged Hispanic woman was sobbing and rocking back and forth uncontrollably. She was ignoring comforting words from her family so I asked if I could help. I learned that this woman had been coming every day to get financial assistance, but would break down emotionally and not be able to complete the process. She had lost her husband in this attack and mere words could not dispel her grief.

I did my best to console her but as I left I felt I had little if any success. A couple of hours later, while making rounds, I saw this woman again. This time she was smiling and even laughing. I wondered what made the difference and then I saw that she had her hands buried deep in the fur of a grieving dog. With his head in her lap she was actually stroking and caressing it while temporarily putting her own grief aside. I noticed a slight wag of the dog's tail and I left with a little lighter heart. I'm not sure who benefited most on that occasion, the widow, the dog or myself.

Teddy bears have always been regarded as a child's comfort toy and many of us still have our children's

I have witnessed families crying from hearts overflowing with grief...

first special bears saved in an attic, or tucked away in a closet. My two sons' bears are sights to see. Jamie's bear is missing an eye, an ear and has hair pulled out. Randy's is so worn it is barely recognizable. Even in their dismal condition the memories and love are still there.

At Pier 94, teddy bears of all shapes, sizes and colors were being given out to anyone directly affected by this attack. Old and young alike were given these symbols of love and they seemed greatly appreciated. I took six special Red Cross bears from my local chapter with the thought of finding just the right children to give them to. They were adorable dark-brown bears wearing little red vests. The vests were embroidered with X's and O's, representing hugs and kisses.

Since I only had six with me, I would have to depend on my inner feelings for direction.

As I mentioned earlier, all non-security entrants were given peel-off stickers to wear denoting "Family" or "Volunteer." I had decided that during the day I would look for the children with tags on their little shirts that said "family." I soon saw a sweet-looking little girl being held by the hand as she was escorted by her crying mother. The little girl was restless and fussing so I asked permission to give her a teddy bear. After receiving permission, I handed her this special teddy bear and immediately a smile spread from ear to ear. As the family passed my aid station several times that day, my heart was touched as I saw her clutching her little teddy bear, grinning from ear to ear and waving to me. Later in the day I gave a second teddy bear out to another crying child. On this my first full workday, two of these little bears found a special home and I knew I had made the right choice.

As I completed my first day, I have witnessed families crying from hearts overflowing with grief and others bringing in DNA samples to begin the arduous task of identifying their relative's remains. I have seen dogs that were depressed from the smell of death give wet doggy kisses to the tear-stained cheeks of mourning victims. I have given teddy bears to two children that will never again feel their father's arms around them, play games with them, or watch them leave for their first day of school.

Through my tear-filled eyes I saw friend supporting friend, stranger hugging stranger and while still in the grip of the worst disaster this city has known, I heard them share words of encouragement, hope and faith. Today in my own eyes I had given out little, but I had truly received much. I witnessed firsthand the strength of the American people.

Vennie, Bert and I walked back to our hotel after a long workday and we were all emotionally drained. I went to my room, curled up under the bed cover and let my tears flow. The words "I'm a nurse, I can handle it" seemed so distant after only one day on the job and I still have 19 more to go.

Day 4

If I count the first half-day of work following orientation, this was my third day on this site. I must confess I had expected a lighter emotional assignment, but in the great scheme of things, there was a reason I am here. To that end I did my best to ease the load of whomever I came in contact with. My prayer was that I not miss an opportunity.

One bright spot today was when word spread that Mariah Carey was coming to visit. I don't keep up with the music world like some, but I had heard that Mariah had recovered recently from an emotional crisis of her own. I thought, *What a wonderful thing for her to do.*

As Bert and I were making our rounds, we passed a little girl approximately 6 years of age sitting in the Red Cross waiting area. A Red Cross mental-health worker was sitting with her, giving her words of encouragement. From what I overheard, I detected that the little girl was having a difficult time dealing with the loss of a parent. It is so hard to see children confronted with this type of loss and she was on my mind as we moved about the facility.

Bert and I completed our rounds, restocked the cart and started another trip. On the second trip I noticed the same little girl holding her teddy bear and smiling. Bert and I stopped the cart, and spoke with the little girl.

"Did you see Mariah Carey?" I asked her. Boy did she smile big on that.

"Yes," she replied, "I even shook her hand."

"You shook Mariah Carey's hand?" I responded excitedly, "Can I touch the hand that Mariah Carey touched?" I further inquired, hoping to make her feel extra special.

"No," she said as she shook her head. "But you can touch my teddy bear right here," as she indicated a spot on its head. "You see, I have to wash my hands when I take my bath each night, so I put her handprint on my Teddy bear's head. He doesn't have to have a bath, and I will always have her hand print." With her consent I gently and respectfully touched the top of this little bear's head. Oh Mariah, you can't imagine the joy that you have brought this little girl today. I wish that you could somehow know. You truly were a volunteer today.

Again at the end of this day, Vennie, Bert and I walked back to the hotel we now referred to as home. We shared the stories of people that we realized were starting to become our people. Has it only been two full days? I have dealt with more sadness than one person usually deals with in a lifetime. Again, I crawled into bed, covered up and cried as I waited for my nightly call from my husband, Roy. I felt that my emotional plate, full when I left home, was now almost empty. How do those workers cope who have toiled day and night since September 11th?

Day 5

This morning I watched a news program while dressing for work, and I was appalled at one segment being shown. When many people in Afghanistan saw the devastation on their televisions, they started singing, shouting and dancing in the streets. They were celebrating our loss and I saw men throwing candy out to the throng of people as if they were in a parade. What a contrast. Two different approaches to the same event, with one side rejoicing, the other side grieving.

Today a congressman from New York came by my workstation to shake my hand and thank me for my part in this recovery effort. Almost daily we see dignitaries from around the world coming here to pay their respects. We know immediately when one is coming because the Secret Service usually arrives first. They are easily identifiable because they all wear little earphones and they spread out quickly looking throughout the building. Usually about 10 show up at a time, and we immediately know something notable is about to happen. Someone at home asked my husband,

Roy, if he was worried about me. "Why?" he replied, "she has more top security around her than Fort Knox."

Today was a real trial for me. I woke up with a splitting headache, a slight fever, and all over achiness, but I forced myself to go to work. My emotions were raw after the last three days and I should have realized my day was not going to improve. But one can hope.

Shortly after my arrival at Pier 94, a 59-year-old man, who appeared much older than his biological age, came walking over to our aid station. His shoulders were slumped, and he had dark circles under his eyes. Since I did not have a patient at that time, I offered to help and he accepted. In the next few minutes he revealed this all too familiar story. He had been a trader and had barely escaped with his life. He told of seeing and hearing people jumping to their deaths, and the scenes and sounds were now haunting him in his sleep. In fact he was getting little sleep and it was taking a toll on his health. He said when he did attempt to sleep, he had recurring dreams of the

He told of seeing and hearing people jumping to their deaths, and the scenes and sounds were now haunting him in his sleep.

Tons of cement and steel remind me of the rubble from cities that were bombed during World War II.

MARY STEPHENS, R.N.

people jumping to their deaths, getting up, going back in the building and jumping again.

Thus far he had been unable to break the cycle and was asking for medication to get through his nights of terror. As tears flowed down both our faces, I leaned over and embraced him. For a moment our tears mingled and then I gently I escorted him to an onsite volunteer psychiatrist who could dispense the necessary medication. As I left him I sent up a prayer for this devastated man.

With the announcement of the

With the news of the collapse of the Twin Towers, medical personnel from all over New York City had rushed to the area to give medical aid.

collapse of the Twin Towers, medical personnel from all over New York City had rushed to the area to give aid. As a result of the massive loss of life and the helplessness felt by those offering their services, many medical personnel were also going through a form of depression. One of the heads of departments at Bellevue Hospital in New York City decided to send some of the interns and residents to Pier 94 to assist in our first-aid station. This seemed to help them and it certainly helped us. For the duration of my stay we turned to these generous people often. The doctors could write prescriptions and do consults right there, and they stayed busy the whole time. I was touched by the caring manner in which they treated the most minor complaints. Many were referred to the ER but most were taken care of on site.

Each day brought new challenges and each night brought more tears. I always waited for the calls from home, calls that would lift my spirits and refill my plate. By this time I was having a difficult time sleeping. After the experiences of the day I would lie in bed, rehash the stories and feel the renewed burden of "my people's" pain. Then I would cry out to God for answers as I struggled for needed rest.

UNITED WE CAME

Day 6

My day started with another brisk walk to work with my friends. This has been so beneficial since Vennie is a mental health worker and Bert, a sister nurse. They understood, for they were experiencing some of the same feelings. Today I referred three patients to St. Luke's Hospital, 2-3 miles from Pier 94. One of them was especially memorable.

He needed transportation to the hospital and had no means of getting there. He had cardiomegaly, which is medical terminology for an enlarged heart. Prior to the attack he was on medication, but was now unemployed and couldn't afford the prescription. This would normally not have been a problem as I had confirmed his medications with his pharmacist and Red Cross policy is to pay the expenses. I had been writing payment vouchers and would have been willing to do so again, but the visiting doctor wanted him seen at the ER for more extensive evaluation. This man had walked three blocks from the bus stop just to get here and was obviously in no condition to walk back. Cabs were not allowed to drive up to Pier 94 due to heightened security and I was in a dilemma. *No problem*, I thought, I would ask one of the policemen to escort him to the hospital.

Our nursing station was situated right between the two main entrances. As people came in the family entrance, there is a small room to the left that is presently being used by the police department. Sensing a solution, I marched confidently into the office and asked one officer to point out the "sweetest" policeman in the office. Two men pointed to each other and almost simultaneously replied, "he is." I chose the one that looked the sternest and started to turn on the remnants of my southern charm. I have lived in Redding, Calif., for 27 years, but my southern roots were sure

to pay off, or so I thought! I presented the situation and asked sweetly for a ride for my patient.

"Absolutely not!" the officer replied, "If he is so sick call an ambulance."

"But Sir," I explained, "he doesn't need an ambulance, just a ride." I further intoned, "Why should the taxpayers pay for an ambulance when you could give him a ride?"

He responded that it is against the rules. I thought, *Boy, have I lost touch with my southern roots.* Not easily discouraged I decided I would give it another chance.

"Sir," I said, "I can't believe what I am hearing. I left my husband [a man who can't cook] for three weeks, and we are supposed to be in New England enjoying the fall colors right now. But no, I left it all to come here and help your people, and you can't even give this man a short ride?"

I waited expectantly as he looked down at me, then said "All right, go get him, but hurry up." What a relief! I hadn't lost my touch completely but it needed some work. I quickly went around the corner, grabbed the patient's hand and hurried him back to the policeman's office. There were more officers in the room when I returned with him.

"Thank you," I said, "Here he is." The officer who had agreed looked over to his superior who had just entered the room and then sat at his desk.

I left it all to come here and help your people, and you can't even give this man a short ride?

The commanding officer then turned to me and quickly said, "Nothing doing, we are not taking you to the ER."

"But he said he would," I flared back, pointing to the first officer.

"Well I am his boss and we are not going to break the rules."

Oh no, I thought, *here we go again*. This was going to be an even bigger challenge.

"But Sir," and then I proceeded to recite the previous winning lines. I smiled, I begged, and I put the best guilt trip on him I could muster.

Finally out of desperation he replied, "Oh all right, but only if a nurse goes with him. I don't want him having a heart attack in the car. It could cause a lot of trouble, since we're bending the rules."

"But Sir," I replied, " I am a nurse."

"Really?" he asked. I could not believe that he would doubt my word. After my stellar performance, I actually had to go and get my boss to come verify that I was a nurse and was qualified to ride with the client. I let them know that I had never ridden in a police car before and that this would be a treat. The officer seemed surprised.

"Really?" he asked. "I guess that you want lights and sirens too?"

My answer to him was, "Why not? I want the royal treatment."

Although hope was waning, the search continued. By the wrap-up day, only 289 whole bodies were recovered.

UNITED WE CAME

So in conclusion, my patient was taken to the hospital in the back of the police car, with me sitting and smiling along side.

On the ride back, the young officer was told by his commander to give me the royal treatment. In the future I won't comment about officers using their red lights to get through traffic for personal reasons for today I got the royal treatment. When I returned, I went to the commander and gave him a big hug and kiss on his cheek right in front of his men. His face turned red, and I said coyly, "Before I leave you are going to need me." Well I am not

How do you respond to a woman whose glasses broke during her collapse when given the news that her daughter was missing?

a prophet, but I knew the flu bug was going around and no one was immune. Sure enough, before I returned home, the commander came to me and sheepishly stuck his hand out for cold medicine. I could not help myself and with a grin on my face as I handed him the medication, I had to say, "I told you so."

Today I also talked with a young man in the National Guard Reserves. He was scared that he would have go to war and I could not give him much assurance that he would not. As I looked at him and realized that he is younger than my own sons, I felt empathy for his mother, knowing how I would feel if he was my son.

Today a lady came needing a replacement set of eyeglasses. Red Cross has a plan where they will replace glasses and provide eye exams after receiving proof of a disaster-related loss. While I explained this to her, she was searching through her purse. In moments she pulled out the receipt for the DNA sample brought in for her daughter who was missing. That was not what I wanted or expected to see. After handing me the receipt, she showed me two pictures of her daughter. She was very attractive and with her broad smile she appeared to be flirting with the camera as the pictures were snapped. I held the pictures in my hands as I ran my finger over her face. Tears were brimming in her mother's eyes.

How do you respond to this? I wondered. How do you respond to a woman whose glasses broke during her collapse when given the news that her daughter was missing? I gave her another gentle hug and signed the Red Cross Disbursement Order that would pay for the new glasses. As she walked away I mentally placed myself in her shoes and shared her grief as my own. By this date there was not really much hope of finding survivors. I went to my hotel room that night and repeated the cycle started my first full day on this assignment. I curled up in bed, relived the day's activities and waited for my support calls. I really needed to touch home base.

UNITED WE CAME

Day 7

My flu symptoms reached a peak today, but I knew I was needed so I crawled out of bed and went to work anyway. After taking a look at me, my supervisor at Pier 94 sent me straight back to the hotel. This time I crawled in bed and slept the day and night away. It was a blessing because I really needed a break from the physically long hours, but mostly a break from the sadness and despair that was all around.

United We Came

Day 8

Today was my assigned day off. Since I had been off sick yesterday, I called in and offered to come in to work to make up the lost time. I was told to enjoy this day and report in on the 10th as scheduled. With this matter settled, I went back to bed for several more hours. When I awoke, I dressed and joined my friends Kathleen McCommons and Bert who were also off on this day.

Working with the Red Cross can be very rewarding, but, depending on the assignment, it can also be very tiring. We are given two days off for every three weeks worked and I had decided to use this time to refill my emotional plate. To show its appreciation, the City of New York was responding to the volunteers with open arms. The Olive Garden Italian Restaurant was giving free meals with proof of ID, the Grey Line Transportation Company was giving free bus tours, and the Circle line was giving free waterway tours. We decided that we would take advantage of everything we could before returning to the pressures of

UNITED WE CAME

Pier 94. For several hours we thoroughly enjoyed seeing this great city. We savored the food that we purchased at the corner deli, took advantage of the museum of natural history and in the evening we accepted the gracious gift of a Broadway play from a local theatre. Yes, I love New York and this is a powerful statement coming from a country girl. I have had a good day. I wonder what tomorrow will bring?

The Statue of Liberty, a beacon of freedom for 122 years, still stands tall in New York Harbor.

United We Came

Day 9

Today was more of the same. We treated minor illnesses and irritated eyes, checked blood pressures and did some mental-health counseling. One middle-aged firefighter came and sat down at my lunch table to talk with me. He estimated that 1,000 children would only have one parent this Christmas due to the events of 9-11. This concerned me so I asked what my home city of Redding could do.

Reaching over to the many cards and letters on the table, he replied, "Ask them to send us cards. Words of thanks and encouragement let us know that we haven't been forgotten."

In our staff dining room our tables are supplied with one to two dozen letters and homemade cards from people all over the United States. Churches, school students and teachers from around the country mailed these to us to lift our spirits. Most of us would pick them up at mealtime and read the messages. Sometimes we would collectively try to determine what the picture depicted or its special meaning. Many of these precious pictures were from toddlers or preschoolers doing their best to draw and share their heartfelt messages, and we certainly didn't want to miss their meaning. I have heard both policemen and firemen reading these notes aloud to others sitting with them at the dinner tables. All the notes were greatly appreciated and many tears were shed while reading them. Surely I have shed a lifetime of tears on this trip.

A mother came in today confident that her 30-year old daughter was going to be found alive. Her reasoning was that her daughter ate properly, exercised daily and lived right. She was not ready to give up hope and I was not ready to dispel that hope. Everyone needs an anchor to cling to.

I had a boost today when the man I rode with to the hospital came back and thanked me for getting him to the emergency room. His condition was appropriately treated and he gave me a big hug and thank you. Appreciation is the merit badge every volunteer works for, and today I received one.

Tonight, at ten o'clock I answered a knock on my hotel door and the doorman was standing there holding a bouquet of a dozen long-stem red roses. On the card was written, "There's no baby like my baby." It was from Roy. He knew I needed a special touch from home and I was so excited to get them.

Day 10

It is October 11th, the one-month anniversary of the terrorist attacks. A voice came over the intercom system this morning asking all to observe a moment of silence. All discourse came to a halt as the mournful sound of a lone bagpipe played the tune "Amazing Grace." As people stood quietly and reverently I wondered if those from other nations knew the song.

They must have, for tears were streaming down many faces as I looked around. Then I remembered that the shedding of tears is a common daily occurrence in this place, so I could not be sure. I could only hope they understood the song's beautiful message. I would never again hear this song with out being taken back in my feelings to this day.

Today I had my first request for funeral money. A young woman having just miscarried wanted to know if Red Cross would help her with burial expenses. Her husband was among the presumed dead and by burying the fetus she felt she would have a part of him to visit and mourn.

Another mother had come to our first-aid station and mentioned that her son's foot had been recovered. She seemed at peace that she could at least have closure now. As I heard this I thought, *Dear God, what a courageous soul that can find relief in the recovery of a foot.* I remembered the feet of my children when they were babies. I would kiss their little pink toes, tweak them and say, "This little piggy went to the market, this little piggy stayed home, this little piggy had roast beef, this little piggy had none, and this little piggy would cry wee-wee-wee all the way home." I would snuggle the little foot and rock back and forth and end the game with a smacking kiss.

Did this mother do the same at one time? I have come to realize in a very small way what it must have been like in wartime. It must have been almost unbearable to the families waiting at home for official word of the loved-one's fate. I can only hope that this experience in New York is the closest I will ever have to come.

After work several of us decided to unwind by going to another Broadway play. Many plays had reduced prices for volunteer workers and since entertainment was a good stress reliever it seemed like the thing to do. We did not realize that getting a taxi after the play was over at 11 p.m. it would be almost impossible, but we soon found out. After trying to hail a cab for what seemed like eternity, we decided to walk. The air was cold and windy and we did not have warm clothes on, so we chilled quickly. We soon learned that we could step into alcoves in front of the stores for a minute or two to catch some warmth. We continued this for a few blocks until some kind soul informed us we were going the wrong direction. With that profound knowledge we decided to take a bus.

We all breathed a sigh of relief when a bus actually stopped for us. We quickly boarded and began rummaging through our purses for the fare. Unbeknownst to us, each patron is required to have the correct change and we only had bills. After a few minutes of trying to solve our dilemma, the young bus driver told us to sit down because he needed to move on and not get behind on his schedule. How to get change now became our focus. An elderly man sitting across from us sat quietly with a twinkle in his eye watching us frantically scrounge through our purses. Some women have a way of getting giddy or snappy when tired and stressed and our group fit the first category nicely. As we began to laugh, the elderly gentleman spoke up and told us that we could ask the other passengers for help. With that information in hand we asked for help and the other riders started searching to find change for us.

We were touched by their kindness,

I have come to realize in a very small way what it must have been like in wartime.

UNITED WE CAME

even though we eventually found enough change between the four of us.

As we exited the bus at our destination, I turned to the group of people waiting to board the bus and with out-stretched arms exclaimed, "Did you know that you have to have correct change to ride these buses?" With that all four of us erupted in deep belly laughter right there on the street corner. It was good therapy for us and I am so glad that there was no identifiable connection with Red Cross on our persons. It seemed like ages since we had anything to laugh about. In reality it had only been a few days.

I couldn't wait to get back to my room to call Roy and share the day and the evening. I belted out another hearty laugh when I found out that Roy's e-mails to our family and friends were being signed "Home alone."

Now, like an established ritual, I wondered what tomorrow would bring me as I lay my head down to sleep. I am such an impatient person. My husband always says, "Mary don't wish your life away." I really should listen to him more often.

The smoldering ruins of the Twin Towers are reminiscent of the Coliseum in Rome, Italy, both symbols of sadness, death and destruction.

UNITED WE CAME

Day 11

The news story for today was about the first case of anthrax in New York City. I have had many people come up offering excuses to get Cipro. One man came and showed me a cold sore on his lower lip completely convinced that he had anthrax. Since he wouldn't take my word for it, I had the doctor examine him. His anthrax scare proved baseless and he ended up with a tube of lip balm.

One of the more unusual requests was for shoe insoles and we began saving them for the rescue workers because we didn't have many. One tall, red-haired Irish policeman came to me for treatment of some painful blisters. After I had him sit in a chair, he took his shoes off and I saw that his socks were bloodied. I had him take them off and found that both of his heels had deep, bloody sores. He had ruined his shoes working at Ground Zero and his new pair had created blisters while breaking in. Going back on the job and working the extra hours had certainly taken its toll on his feet. These men were working long, hard hours due to the shortage of officers and their emotional obligation to their fallen brothers. I told the policeman to come back twice a day and I would treat his feet for him. After a hearty thank you and big hug, he went his way.

True to his promise, he did come back daily for treatment. In the meantime I had carefully searched through our supplies and found one pair of insoles. To keep them safe, I hid them in a cardboard box filled with medications until I could give them to him. He was so happy when I handed the newfound insoles to him that he immediately sat down, opened the package, cut them to size with borrowed scissors and inserted them into his shoes. Before I returned home to California this thoughtful young man brought me a special T-shirt. During my stay, many gifts in the form of pins, caps and shirts were being given to us nurse volunteers as tokens of appreciation. Each gift holds a special place in my heart for the one from whom it was received.

The recovery workers, were a hardworking lot, but they managed to find a little time for humor. Today during my rounds with the medication cart, I was "set up" by several young firemen. I was told there were a couple of men suffering from the "Irish flu" over in the fire section and asked if I could help. I immediately felt sympathy for them as a nasty virus was going around. I wheeled my cart to the curtained section where the men were resting and proceeded to talk with them. Trying to sound upbeat in a dismal situation, I pulled the curtains apart and started offering them nursing advice. One young man turned to the other, and with a twinkle in his eye, started describing his symptoms while the other fireman tried not to laugh. After receiving my verbal list of instructions, they both burst out laughing and said all they needed was aspirin for their hangover. I had encountered my first case of "Irish flu," and I had to laugh at myself for my naiveté. It was good to laugh for it was much needed therapy.

Late today we had a bomb scare. While caring for our clients we noticed a military guard with arms outstretched herding a group of people past us. "Come

I had encountered my first case of "Irish flu," and I had to laugh at myself for my naiveté.

quickly!" he urged. "And don't bring anything." I grabbed the Red Cross vouchers, the equivalent of blank checks, and quickly hid them in boxes behind the curtain on the back wall. I then hurried outside with the rest of my co-workers who, like myself, had no idea what the urgency was. We were told to cross the street and continue walking another two blocks to where the buses stop. Apparently something suspicious was noticed and as a precaution we were all evacuated.

After the all clear was given, some workers requested permission to leave early and go to their hotel

UNITED WE CAME

rooms rather than return to the evacuated building. Since our belongings were in the building, we needed to return to retrieve them. One of the young doctors from Bellevue Hospital was very uneasy about returning and he kept saying, "I don't like the feel of this, I don't want to go back." Attempting to find a solution, I offered to retrieve his backpack for him. At first I did not take him seriously, but when I asked a second time, "Did you really mean it, are you really uneasy?" he assured me that he was. After he hesitantly decided to return for his backpack, I tried to make light of the situation by turning to him and saying, "Don't worry, if something happens, all us old nurses will throw our bodies on you to protect you." He burst out laughing, returned for his backpack, and then left.

Bert, Vennie and I had much to talk about on our way to our hotel. This day was somewhat different from the others, and I had a lot to share with Roy when he called. Also tonight, I had another great surprise. The employees at Roy's and my company sent a large flower arrangement and words of praise and encouragement.

Every day the workers were faced with tons of mangled metal. Metal that entombed thousands of precious loved ones. In all, 1,610,852 tons of debris came from the wreckage.

UNITED WE CAME

Day 12

I was starting to wake up during the night and not be able to go back to sleep. I remembered the warning they gave me during orientation about our own mental health. They had said we might need to talk to a mental-health counselor at some point during or after our stay. I remembered scoffing at this, but now I am beginning to think that some counseling might not be a bad idea after all. Then I wondered, What if someone finds out? Will I be relieved and sent home? *I didn't want that, so I decided to ignore my own needs.*

One of my challenges today was in helping a young mother who was trying desperately to put her life back together. She and her husband were recently separated and she was staying in another state with family members when the WTC attack occurred. Her husband was a victim of the attack but she had been unable to obtain proof. A family member had driven her to Pier 94 to apply for financial assistance and request help in getting a death certificate. She came in carrying a small brown paper bag that contained her marriage license, social security card and the birth certificates of their children. I found out that she was already under a doctor's care and was sent to me because of concerns with her blood pressure. After determining that her blood pressure was within acceptable limits, I sat with her a few moments and listened to her story.

Her husband had made a practice of calling her on the phone every day of their marriage and continued this ritual after their separation. She was already shouldering deep feelings of guilt, and his death was more than she could handle. She said that she felt as though this was just a dream and eventually she would wake up to find him calling her again. Oh, how many times I have heard similar story lines since I arrived here. She expressed that her life was not worth living and that she was having a hard time seeing a tomorrow. I listened quietly as I watched her body tremble and shudder. I knew that her problem was beyond the scope of my training so I told her that we had a special department offering mental-health and spiritual counseling.

At first she refused but her family member was with her and also encouraged her to seek further help. She turned to me requesting that I accompany her. She said she didn't want the family member there to hear her private thoughts and feelings, but yet she didn't want to be alone. I assured her I would not leave her till she felt ready, and then I took her in search of my friend Vennie.

Unfortunately, Vennie was unavailable because she was already with a client, so I asked for another counselor and was directed to one.

After introducing my client to the counselor, I asked if she really wanted me to stay with her. She must have felt at ease with this worker because she said that I could leave and she would be fine. She was then taken into the quiet area set aside for private counseling.

Roy called me at work today, which is unusual. He said that he was concerned for me, and that he could tell by my voice that it was time for me to seek some counseling of my own. I assured him that I would and from that point forward I searched for an opportune time.

I now had both my sisters and my husband telling me I sounded like I needed some help.

When you are a volunteer and working with other volunteers, you feel like part of a big family. You work together, eat together, take days off together and share experiences with each other. Without actually planning it, you soon realize that you have become part of a support system. This was my first out-of-state job and my desire to prove I could handle it caused me to forgo the full benefits that the system offered. I now had both my sisters and my husband telling me I

UNITED WE CAME

sounded like I needed some help. *If it was that obvious during a telephone conversation then maybe they are right,* I thought.

On a side note, I noticed that the workers and volunteers in this building are all coming down with the flu virus. I feel its main cause is lack of rest and stress. Bert and I have been giving out hundreds of bottles of water and dispensing all kinds of over-the-counter medication to combat the effects.

Later in the day, I spotted a mental-health worker walking by our first-aid station. I had been thinking about my family's concern, so I called out and asked if he had a minute to talk. We spent the next 30 minutes

Aside from civilians, the ranks of the firefighters suffered the most, with 443 losing their lives.

talking together and sharing the same box of tissues.

During our conversation he said, "Mary, I have been asked so many times by so many people, have you seen the big hole?" The disaster is played over and over on television and is referred to as the big hole. "Mary, the hole is not the empty space at the WTC, the hole is really the emptiness inside each and every person that is walking around here. It's an empty space that can't be filled. Not only the loss of life, but of lively hood, a means of providing for ones family." As he continued, I sat listening to him as if under a spell. After a while he stood, wiped his tear-stained face and told me that tomorrow he was finally getting a day off, his first in two weeks. He said he was going to the park and would just sit there watching the birds.

We both agreed that the atmosphere here today had been emotionally heavy and time off was a necessity. Then we hugged each other and went back to work.

I had a pick-me-up today, and I couldn't wait to tell Roy. A troop of girl scouts from Lancaster, Pa., made cute refrigerator magnets and sent them for Red Cross volunteers. Each magnet was made in the shape of a red-painted cross, and had a white heart in the center. Painted in the center of the heart was the number "2001" and the words "thank you." The girls had made a little gift box out of craft paper and hand stamped little designs all over it. Nestled inside each box was a magnet with a hand-written note. The note was a personal thank you to Red Cross workers for helping. The gifts were limited in number and could only be given to nurses that had been members of the Girl Scouts or Brownies. I was grateful that as a little girl I was a member of this organization and was able to receive one of these gifts. My special gift was made by Briana Smith, a fourth grader from Pennsylvania. It means as much to me as would a jewel-encrusted antique.

Yes, I have much to share with Roy when he calls, but I don't want him or my family to worry about me.

I will survive this ordeal because I have the support of my family, my friends and my God.

Day 13

The days are starting to run together but the stories, although similar, are unique to the individual. Today I met another of the many heroes, one that will always stand out in my heart. His name is Ira Sapir and he granted permission to use his true name in telling his story. He is a metal worker and when he heard the news of the buildings collapsing, he immediately responded to the "call of duty."

Ira went to the Chelsea pier where one of his friends operates a tugboat. Wanting to help in any way they could, they started transporting masses of frightened people from Manhattan Island to New Jersey. The next morning Ira went to the disaster site with his metal-working tools, ready to assist in recovery efforts. At that point, he had only one thought in mind, and that was to help rescue as many missing as possible.

I did not meet Ira at a deli, a Broadway play, or even walking to work. I met Ira at Pier 94 when he came to my first-aid station seeking

UNITED WE CAME

help. When Ira arrived at the scene on September 12th, he immediately went to work with his acetylene torch, cutting through the twisted metal. He worked side by side with a horde rescue workers frantically searching for any signs of life. Ira did not punch a time clock for he was not on anyone's payroll. He continued working tirelessly for five more days before suffering a debilitating injury when a large metal beam collapsed on his shoulder. He was now unable to work and had no insurance coverage to pay mounting medical expenses. I stood listening to Ira's story and asked for verification. He reached into his pocket and pulled out a packet of pictures. "Yes, I have verification." he said. A small group of nurses and volunteer

Volunteers from all walks of life joined the monumental clean-up effort while putting their own lives on hold. Words of thanks are not enough.

doctors immediately gathered around to see his pictures and hear his story.

I wanted so much to personally promise Ira that his problems would be solved, but we have procedures to follow. I took Ira to my superior and left the final decision in her hands. After he left I thought, here is a true hero, another who willingly put his life at risk to help his people. In my heart his people are fast becoming my people, people that are in my presence at Pier 94 by day, and in my mind at night.

Nighttime is just like daytime without sunshine, and as an adult I realize this. But childhood impressions have a way of hanging on, and I had developed a fear of the dark during my youth. I would lie in bed at night and imagine seeing the furniture moving or shapes forming in the shadows. It didn't help matters when my two sisters would sneak under my bed at night and gently push my mattress up and down. The next day they would tell me it was the devil and I believed them. They said he was after me for my previous day's mischief and I knew it had to be true. I still wonder why he didn't take me away knowing all I had done.

Fear of the dark was secondary, as I lay awake alone in my hotel room. My primary focus was on the plight of the people here in New York; my people. When did they become my

Here is a true hero, one who willingly put his life at risk to help his people.

people? I don't really know, but I couldn't wait for calls from my family to share with them about "my people." As a nurse, I could not share their names for confidentiality reasons, but I could share their tragic stories. It seems that all burdens are lighter when they are shared.

1:00 a.m.

Tonight I fell asleep sometime after midnight and was awakened at 12:35 a.m. by a call from the hotel bellman. He said that he had a delivery and it couldn't wait until morning. My thoughts started running wild as they often do, and I wondered, *Did I drop some ID? What could it be?* Five minutes later he knocked on my door and I greeted him in my old, red-plaid flannel pajamas with holes in them, my hair disheveled, and a confused look on my face. In his hand was a huge bouquet of flowers and I instantly perked up. It had red roses, white lilies, white daisies, green fern and was an armful. Attached to the vase was a darling, tiny teddy bear dressed in a little crocheted vest with a green bow on its head. The note said, "Mary, we appreciate you. From your Red Cross board and staff." I truly felt their love and support, and it was needed. The teddy bear was their way of sending a message of comfort. I knew it was a way of sending me hugs, as most of us at my local chapter in Redding are huggers. Of course I had to immediately call my husband and my sisters to tell them. After I finished bragging, I lay back in bed and pulled the window shade up to let a little of the outside light shine in. I wanted to see my flowers during the night when I would wake up, as I often did.

UNITED WE CAME

Day 14

Today I had another day off. Normally I would need to go to the laundry, but not today. I have been washing my clothes out in the sink at night and they have been dry by morning. A quick pass with the room iron and my clothes looked fine.

Bert and I talked over our options and decided to take advantage of "fine dining week." "Fine dining" is offered once a year and allows people to go to the fancy, expensive restaurants for a minimal price. We felt we could handle this, and decided to dress up and give it a try. Until now we had been eating most of our meals and snacks at pier 94 with no complaints.

Today, however, a fancy meal sounded like it was up our alley. So, in anticipation, we donned long dresses, high heels, and hailed a cab.

The cabby dropped us off at La Cirque, and we had an absolutely fantastic meal. We sat next to two locals and visited as we dined. We then took a complimentary evening cruise around Manhattan. During the cruise, the ferry stopped in front of the WTC area and the crew turned off the motor. With the multitude of lights illuminating the area, one couldn't help but see the plumes of smoke wafting toward us from the burning mass of rubble. The jagged beams and severely damaged buildings appeared as great monuments leaning at angles that one would expect to topple in a slight breeze. The night air was filled with the engine sounds of many large cranes and earthmovers. Contrary to appearance, the skeletal frames would not easily topple, for it would take months of round-the-clock manpower to remove this rubble from its standing place.

Through the coming months, piece by precarious piece, they would gently pry it away, much like a comforter tenderly pulling the fingers of a grieving mother away from her child's casket.

Across from us to the right we could see the Statue of Liberty. Standing tall like a proud mother with her lit torch held high, she seemed

The jagged beams and severely damaged building appeared as great monuments leaning at angles that one would expect to topple in a slight breeze.

The precarious beams, all that was left standing of the magnificent buildings, were added to the rubble, which averaged 6,148 tons per day.

MARY STEPHENS, R.N.

to be lighting the way for the rescue workers. The National Anthem came to my heart and, as I hummed the song, I was proud that all through the night, the flag was still there. I consider myself to be a tender-hearted person, but I can't remember experiencing the intensity and duration of these feelings before. I can only imagine what the residents of New York City must feel.

After I got home to my hotel, my messages indicated that my son James and Ginny Yost, a friend from my church, had called to let me know that I wasn't forgotten. Once again I am having a difficult night getting to sleep. It is after 1 a.m. and, as usual, I need to be up at 5:00 to prepare for work.

Day 15

Today I wrote out vouchers for several people to get their eyeglasses replaced. While fleeing the attack area their glasses had fallen off and gotten trampled. We are now seeing more clients that are here because they are unemployed and need financial assistance. The Red Cross is helping with rent, food, utilities and clothes. One middle-aged man came in showing signs of depression. He wanted to share his story, and I encouraged him to talk.

He and his best friend were janitors, working in the same building. Over the years they had grown as close as brothers and spent a lot of time together. His friend was 55 and had planned to be married September 15, with my client acting as best man. When evil struck on September 11th, the best friend perished and my client's world collapsed along with the trade center. He was feeling guilty for surviving, as is common in these types of situations. I did my best to console him and talked with him at length. Toward the end he made a positive comment that he was getting strength from seeing America pull together. I immediately thought, *But oh, at what a cost.*

Tonight Bert and I have tickets to see another Broadway play, "Kiss me Kate." We really need to see and hear something humorous. Laughter is truly good medicine. 🏳

Day 16

Today we again basically followed the same routine. We made the rounds with our cart, treated flu symptoms, headaches, dehydration, and gave out smiles and hugs. We are getting good at fooling the people with our facial expressions.

We put forth a big smile on the outside, cry on the inside and hope we can keep up the act until our three-week tour of duty is over. If these dear people could look forward to their problems ending in three weeks, I'm sure their outlook would be much brighter.

A young fireman came up to my friend Beverly for first-aid treatment. Beverly is a volunteer nurse who took a leave of absence from her regular job to come and help. I was standing next to Bev as this young man was talking to her, so I couldn't help but overhear. He was saying that he had lost 32 friends, and had already attended 20 of their funerals. He said he didn't think he could attend another one because he was emotionally drained. My heart went out to him. I am 52 and I have not attended more than seven or eight funerals in my life. He is growing up fast.

Later in the day I was called to help a choking victim who had been eating in the family dining area. When I got there she was still having trouble, but she had an open airway so I just stood by for a while to give assistance if needed.

Walking to the hotel helps clear my mind and gives me needed exercise. Tomorrow will be here all too soon.

Day 17

Again we passed out food, hugs, water and advice. Our day was generally uneventful and that was a blessing. My concern for these people is still running high and I sincerely hope we are making a difference. I feel so helpless in dealing with many of their problems but I will do the best I can.

For our own peace of mind, some of us tried traveling a new route to the rest rooms. We wanted to avoid seeing the pictures on the "walk of bears" because the faces were becoming so familiar. They seemed to stare back at us, reminding us of the many sad stories we had heard. In my case, during the day when I looked at them, I found myself creating mental connections to people I had helped. At night they replayed in my mind and interrupted my sleep.

United We Came

Day 18

The doctors from Bellevue Hospital are such a big help as they continued conducting exams and writing prescriptions. They not only help the clients at Pier 94 but also aid the emergency rooms by keeping them available for true emergencies.

I was asked by my superior to extend my stay another week, so we are considering it. I say "we" because Roy and I have been marriage partners for almost 35 years, and we make our decisions as a team. This is the longest period we have been separated since being married, so I have left the final decision up to him. After all he is the one who doesn't cook.

Of all the days so far, this had been the most emotional day during my tour of duty. Maybe it was a combination of fitful nights with little rest, the emotional aspect of my job, or the moon. Well, doesn't the moon deserve some blame? It does have a reputation to uphold.

I decided to call my sister Margie on my cell phone for a pick-me-up and was just leaving the rest room to return to my first-aid station. The clock showed 9:00 a.m. and the building was filling up fast. As we were talking, a voice came over the PA system asking for the people to stop their business, turn to the nearest flag and show respect in whatever fashion they felt comfortable with. Since there are people of all nationalities represented here, some stood silently while those of us who are Americans covered our hearts with our right hand or saluted.

As I stood with my eyes fixated on "Old Glory" an event transpired that I shall never forget. Over the loudspeaker came the lone voice of a man singing "The Star Spangled Banner." As he sang, I sensed such deep emotion and love in his voice that I scarcely noticed that the tune was not being carried well. My left hand was still holding my cell phone while my sister continued to listen on the other end. Suddenly I felt a wave of emotion overcome me and I could not contain my feelings. It filled me with pride in my country, and thankfulness that I could be here to help my people. The tears started flowing and for most of us they continued throughout the day. As I looked around there were not many dry eyes in the building and no one seemed ashamed to express their emotions.

At the end of the song I made my way to my workstation and began the well-practiced routine. Thirty minutes later, the Red Cross administrator came and asked if I would be willing to help in the family-service area. I agreed to give whatever assistance I could, and the day went downhill from there.

My job assignment in the family-service area was to register clients and verify that they had valid claims for financial assistance. I was told to look for any form of ID that offered proof of their employment related to losses. As always, there were some that understood why they were not qualified and others that would not think twice before trying to fool us. I checked tax records, pay stubs, marriage licenses and any legal documents that would offer the proof I required. I was still struggling with my own emotions as these people came and sat down in front of me. Each family wanted to

Suddenly I felt a wave of emotion overcome me and I could not contain my feelings.

share their situation, and I in turn did my best to console them. I observed that when people realize you are a nurse, they seem to feel comfortable with sharing even the most intimate details.

One interview was with a young man in his late 30s who had immigrated from Mexico to this land of opportunity. His plan was to find employment that would provide for his family both here and back home. He said that hard work, long hours or menial jobs didn't bother him as long as he could remain employed. He came to the service center asking for help with his finances, but his case presented a special challenge. He had

been working in the food-service industry, and the company he worked for was paying him "under the table" in cash. This presented a problem because he had no proof that he had actually worked in this country. He had a local family, an extended family, bills coming in, no food and no visible means of support. I sent him to the immigration section knowing that they would be better qualified to sort this out. I noticed that all the services represented here are cooperating to meet the massive needs of the WTC victims. I know that in situations where I can't help, there are usually other departments that can.

In another scenario we had private chauffeurs coming in by the dozens. Prior to this assignment I never fully realized the number of people out of work as a result of this attack. They included nannies, barbers, waiters, cab drivers, limousine drivers, gardeners, actors, tourist industry workers and the list seems never ending.

Another story came from a 32-year-old man who was standing in my line two hours waiting for his turn. His beautiful suit caught my eye because my son James wears and enjoys expensive clothing. As he sat down I tried to lighten the mood by

There were some that understood why they were not qualified and others that would not think twice before trying to fool us.

complimenting him on his suit. After some small talk I followed by asking for proof of employment, and then his story unfolded.

He told me that he is married and his wife was due to deliver their second child around December 2nd. He had arrived in New York City from Jamaica a number of years ago looking for a better opportunity. He worked hard and had put himself through college. In addition, he had struggled up the employment ladder and had become a securities trader. Now as he sat before me he was beaten down. He started crying and I started crying. I rose up from my chair, leaned over the table between us, and said, "I need a hug." As stated earlier, this became my standard line when I knew my client needed a human touch. It saves face for them

and it helps me cope as well. We clung together and sobbed, oblivious to the line of people observing us.

After we regained control of our emotions, he told me that this was the first time he had actually cried since 9-11. He said that he had escaped with his life by a mere two minutes. As he lifted his head, he looked me in the eye and admitted that he was ashamed to be here asking for charity. He had been using a savings account to live on the past six weeks and was now penniless. He had hoped to quickly find another job but soon realized it was hopeless. It has been estimated that between 100,00 and 200,000 were unemployed as a result of this disaster. I encouraged him to hold his head high and walk tall. I counseled that getting temporary help was nothing to be ashamed of. Before I finished with him I received a big thank you and another big hug.

It was mid afternoon when I suddenly realized that I had cried almost constantly from 9:15a.m. till 2:00 p.m. Most of that time I had been barely able to read the words that I had written on the forms. I had handled 42 clients and at this point realized I couldn't listen to another story or give another hug. My armor had been pierced and I needed help myself. Where was the confident nurse from Redding? She now appeared so foreign to me. I didn't know her anymore. My plate was totally empty, and I had no more to give. My fellow nurses had come by several times with the cart and saw the emotional state that I was in. They urged me to take a break, so I asked to be excused, went to the lunchroom and found a priest and mental-health worker.

I sat down and tried to communicate through my hiccups and tears as they gently started counseling me. They patiently sat with me for 45 minutes as I worked through my emotions, and I needed it desperately. Once I regained control, I was told that I could go back to the first-aid station. I was so emotionally drained that I didn't know for certain if family services didn't need me any longer or they knew I could not handle anymore.

At 4:00 p.m., a woman who appeared to be in her early 30s came by to request aspirin and a small box of tissues that we were handing out. She was crying profusely, so I pushed my own depression aside, gave her a hug and listened to her story. Her brother was a traveling fire-prevention specialist who just happened to stop by the WTC on the morning of September 11th for coffee with a friend. She said friends and family had attended a memorial service this past week, but his body had not yet been recovered.

Today however, she came to post his picture on the wall at the walk of bears and pick up his death certificate. She recounted that until now it seemed as if he was just on one of his out-of-town business trips. As reality sunk in, she was experiencing emotional devastation. She made eye contact and asked if I would like to go see her brother's picture. Yes, I replied, though my mind was saying no, no, no. I can't take anymore.

Today she came to post his picture on the wall and pick up his death certificate.

I walked with her to the "walk of bears" and she pointed out his picture. He was handsome with strawberry-colored hair and blue eyes. He was on the stocky side, but obviously in good shape. Now, because he went for coffee with a friend, he was gone. I reached out my hand and lightly caressed the picture as she continued her story. She told me that they had been to a family gathering in July when she took particular notice of her brother's facial features, the way he walked and his gestures. She went on to tell that her son had an uncanny resemblance to her brother. Each time she sees her son now, she is reminded of her brother. After

UNITED WE CAME

she finished talking, she thanked me for listening, gave me a hug, and apologized for taking me away from the first-aid station.

As I prepared to leave for the day I thought, *This truly is my work. Thank you, God, for my lovely people.* Realizing the severe drain on my own emotional reserves, I reluctantly declined to stay the extra week. I felt a deep sense of guilt. because there are so many that still need help. I still have two days to go, but I know in my heart that once I return home, and my emotional plate is refilled, I will return.

Bert, Vennie and I were walking back to our hotel and I noticed that Vennie was unusually quiet. I said, "Vennie, you haven't said three words, are you O.K.?"

"No," she replied. "This has been the hardest day yet, and I am looking forward to going home."

"I feel the same," I replied. "Today has been my worst day, too." As we continued the walk home in the dark, we shared our own perception of the day's happenings. It was agreed that we sensed a dark cloud hovering over Pier 94 the whole day.

We clung together and sobbed, oblivious to the line of people observing us.

Health issues became a major concern for the rescuers once the smoke cleared, but their lungs didn't. But each went in selflessly and would do it again if necessary.

UNITED WE CAME

Day 19

The young man sang again this morning, and his delivery was just as touching as the day before. I feel so much pride in my country, my volunteer organization and my people here in New York City.

When I arrived at work, a retired physician, who is a Red Cross volunteer, told me that Roy called and seemed upset. I quickly put my belongings under the curtained table and called him. Yes, he was upset because he tried calling me earlier and didn't get an answer. He knew the stress I was under and was frustrated that he could not be here to support me when I needed him. I assured him that I was fine and had decided to return home rather than extend my stay.

Later in the morning an elderly Chinese man with his interpreter came to our first-aid station and sat in one of the exam chairs. He was having a difficult time emotionally and needed a private moment to regain control. I still had one of my special teddy bears hidden in reserve, and I knew when I saw him he was meant to have it.

I reached into its hiding place, retrieved it, squeezed it tight and with a wish and a prayer handed it to him. I asked the interpreter to explain to him that I had only brought six of these special bears to comfort six very special people. I wanted her to tell him that in my heart I knew that he was one of those special people. I stood as she explained this to him in his native language and his face suddenly beamed with joy. As he clutched the bear close to his chest, his eyes crinkled up and, in very broken English,

As he clutched the bear close to his chest, his eyes crinkled up and, in very broken English, he kept repeating, "Thank you, thank you."

he kept repeating, "Thank you, thank you." When was the last time a teddy bear made you happy?

That afternoon a beautiful young woman stopped at our station for some minor first aid. Pinned to the left side of her blouse was a miniature, ornate, silver-colored frame that held a wedding picture. As I looked more closely I observed that she was the bride in the picture and I assumed the man was her husband. She had a day label indicating "family," so I also assumed that her husband was lost in the attack. Intending to offer a word of comfort I said, "What a handsome husband you had." She made direct eye contact immediately and told me with an air of confidence, "He is not dead! He is just missing and he will come home." I smiled and replied that I hoped things would work out for her. After six weeks of digging, I was sure all hope of finding anyone alive had ended. I was obviously wrong. I know that people must come to terms with death and loss in their own way and their own time. I cannot truthfully say what my own reaction would be given similar circumstances.

Toward the end of my shift I could feel the emotional roller coaster picking up downhill speed again. Two elderly ladies stopped by to show us a picture of their missing nephew who was a fireman. Another lady pushing a carriage with a set of twins stopped for cold medicine. The twins were asleep and looked like little cherubs cuddled together without a care in the world. When they are older they will miss the presence of their loving father. One who would have been proud to lend his protective arms to support theirs as they walked down the aisle to be given away in marriage. I still can't grasp the scope of this attack. How could anyone hate so much?

I finished my day by escorting a local volunteer worker to her residence. She said that a large object had fallen on her head, and requested a medical evaluation. After examination by several nurses, we decided that her injuries were not serious and I was asked to escort her home. I was glad to have an opportunity to leave early. I was anxious to get home to Roy, to feel loved, cared for and protected.

UNITED WE CAME

Day 20

After closing out business with the Red Cross I became an ordinary tourist, so I was free to spend the rest of my day as I pleased. I was invited as a guest to an apartment building that was one-and-a-half blocks from Ground Zero, and I accepted the offer.

I was told that the friend's apartment was on one of the lower floors, but the view from the roof was excellent. I had not been able to get a firsthand view of the destruction site, so I was anxious for the opportunity. Another friend and I decided to ride the subway to the apartment location and check it out. It was well worth the trip.

When we arrived, our friend met us in the lobby and escorted us to his apartment. We spent some time visiting, and then he took us to the rooftop. As I looked down and saw the devastation live for the first time, I gasped. Smoke was still billowing up from the rubble, and a huge crane was methodically swinging back and forth picking up the twisted metal. I could hardly believe my eyes.

Our friend said that on the morning of Sept. 11, he heard the crash of the first plane and ran to the roof to see the damage. He was standing in amazement as the second plane hit. As he described the events, a shudder ran through my body and chill bumps covered my arms. He told us that for the first several weeks he was so upset that he could not talk about the experience. After the second plane hit he immediately ran back into his apartment and closed the windows. Then he and his girlfriend fled the area. Now, six weeks later, after rain and high pressure hosing, there is still about a 1/2 inch of cement dust on the window casings, stairs and roof. He was forced to relocate because his girlfriend has cystic fibrosis and could not live in a polluted environment. He shared his binoculars, and as I scanned the area, I noticed a group of uniformed men and workers standing around in a reverent manner. As I focused in I saw an American flag being unfolded and shaken out. *That is strange*, I thought. *There are so many flags all around, why are they unfolding another one?* I dismissed the thought and continued looking about the site for a while longer.

After the rooftop experience, we were taken on a two-hour walking tour complete with historical narration. This was another kind gesture from a local New Yorker. I had met this friendly young man on this trip, and wanting to show kindness and hospitality, he offered to show us the city. In his own way he was saying

Almost every type of heavy equipment imaginable was used at Ground Zero, from large cranes to back hoes, dump trucks to bulldozers.

MARY STEPHENS, R.N.

"thank you" to Red Cross volunteers for lending a hand when help couldn't wait. His thoughtfulness was greatly appreciated.

The mystery of the unfolded flag was solved the next day as I learned that I was witnessing the recovery of eight bodies. In honor of the fallen, the recovery workers would take off their hats, honor them with a salute, and then cover the remains with a shroud of Stars and Stripes. "Oh say, does that star spangled banner yet wave, o'er the land of the free, and the home of the brave."

Day 21

My big day. Home at last. Not to try to forget, but to try and heal and put everything into perspective. I arrived at the airport early and was pulled out of line to be searched. I had no problem with this nor did I have a moment of concern when the announcement came that we were going to be delayed for another hour.

Apparently there was a security concern in coach class and the maintenance crew was unbolting and inspecting under the seats. I was thankful for the extra security in light of the devastation I had just witnessed.

When the plane was finally ready for boarding, I was pulled aside again for a second search. Then, I was given a seat in business class as a thank you for helping in the recovery effort. In addition, I was thanked by the entire cabin crew and even given a bottle of wine to carry home. The funny thing is that we don't drink wine, but I didn't want to offend anyone so I graciously accepted. The wine bottle will look good sitting on my Italian-tiled countertop with a trailing vine hanging down the side.

The flight was long and tiring, but I was going home at last. Even though the plane was running a little behind schedule, I didn't care. I couldn't wait to get home to see my loved ones. As I disembarked and walked through the glass doors, I was surprised to be greeted by a cheering crowd, and to see flash bulbs going off. The news media was there for my homecoming, along with a group of 30 friends holding flowers and balloons and a welcome home poster. The greatest excitement of all came when my eyes landed on Roy. He was proudly holding 21 red roses, one for each day that

I knew then that I would have to go back and help my people.

I had gone, and 21 helium-filled balloons. I rushed to his arms, buried my head in his chest and the torrent of tears flowed once again. This time, though, it was a mixture of sad and happy tears. When he put his arms around me I thought of the many families that would never feel their loved one's arms around them again. I was truly blessed. I could not wait to come home to the love and safety I knew would be waiting for me. Once I arrived and the euphoria subsided, my heart started

Home at last with Roy, I rushed to his arms, buried my head in his chest and the torrent of tears flowed once again. No more frozen dinners for Roy.

MARY STEPHENS, R.N.

missing my people. I couldn't stop thinking about them. As Roy ushered me away to our waiting car, I turned to him and said, "I am so glad to be home, but you know I have to go back." I knew then that I would have to go back and help my people.

Conclusion

What is a hero? Can you become a hero through genetics, or can you learn to be a hero by taking classes at school?

Many rescue and recovery personnel were third- and fourth-generation firefighters and police officers, but that did not make them heroes. Many took classes in rescue and recovery and spent many hours practicing their skills. But this does not make them heroes. They became heroes in their own right when they put the lives of others before that of their own, and the future of their families.

I still keep in touch with Ira Sapir, a hero mentioned in my journal. I would like to quote a portion of one of his letters to me.

"I think the serious problems that will come will not be problems like my shoulder, but problems from the things that we breathed. This seems like the most persistent problem. But with all that being said, we all knew what we were doing, and we all knew the consequences and accepted this.

UNITED WE CAME

I would gladly put myself in that situation again without a second thought, as would almost any other person I know."

It is for courageous people like these that I returned to New York City for another three weeks of service in January. As of this writing, my journey continues. 🏳️

Ira and his friend worked countless hours. It was for people like them and courageous others that I returned for another three weeks of service.

UNITED WE CAME

Afterword

I have been asked about the adjustment after my homecoming. Questions like, How do you feel? Are you going back? Are you glad that you went? My mental response is, Can a football player adequately describe the emotional high of winning the Super Bowl to a fan? *Or,* Can a new mother relate the joy of motherhood to one who has never given birth? *Some things must be experienced to be truly appreciated.*

Yes, I am glad that I went, for my life has been changed. I have learned to place greater value on the small pleasures of life. I am more aware of the sunsets, the birds chirping on a spring day, a visit with a friend. Each day needs to be treated as if might be our last. I have learned many lessons that I would not have learned without going. Those lessons are both humbling and gratifying, but they are not without cost. When I returned, I had emotional adjustments to make. I had difficulty sleeping and often found myself quietly rolling over to the edge of the bed to cry silently for the people that I had left behind. Roy would usually notice my restlessness, scoop me into his arms and ask if I needed to talk. For long periods of time I would need his loving reassurance and patience.

I had trouble focusing on tasks at hand. I would start doing something as simple as cleaning my house and just stop, sit on the couch totally unfocused and not complete the job. I recognized this as depression, but I had more experience treating it in others.

The Red Cross organization is a very caring one. One that cares as much for its volunteers as the clients they serve.

At the beginning of my trip I was told that mental-health counseling was available for the workers as well as their clients. I was encouraged to take advantage of it, and often, if needed. After returning home, a thank you letter was sent expressing appreciation for the time spent helping. Attached was a list of the reactions that are a common occurrence in this type of disaster. It mentioned sleeplessness, change of eating habits, lack of focus, emotional outbursts, as well as others. Post-Traumatic Stress Syndrome is now more than just a condition of the weak.

About the Author

In 1992 Mary graduated from Shasta College with her nursing degree. She now volunteers with the American Red Cross, acting as Supervisor of Disaster Health Services in Shasta, Trinity and Lassen Counties.

In July 2001 Mary received the Clara Barton Award from her chapter of the American Red Cross. This is one of the highest awards given to a volunteer. She also received written commendations from the California State Senate and State Assembly.

When asked for a favorite quote, Mary is quick to reply with two verses from the Bible: "Do unto others as you would have them do unto you," and, "Greater love hath no man than this, that a man lay down his life for a friend."

HOPE FOR THE CHILDREN

I have always had a soft spot for children, and I cannot complete my book without sharing some pictures and letters from them. My granddaughter Alexis occasionally expresses her thoughts for me in the form of hand-drawn pictures and it is always interesting to see the world through a child's mind. Children and youth all across America sent their support in the best way they knew how and I am proud to know that these young people are the future of the United States. By seeing their concern I have greater confidence that our country will be in good hands.

Rose
Red
Love

Dove Peace
White Sign
Freedom America
Blue

Don't blink a tear for madness, Cry a blessed tear for sadness, Give your shadowness a light; Come out send away your fright United we stand and United we'll fall, we are America's blessed, America's tall. Your heart might ache don't stay blank we are united and united we'll stay, forever, forever to this day.

6th grader

A poem above, and a heavenly scene at right. Note the sympathetic weeping clouds and the child-angels below.

Dear America,

People all over the world have been efected by this act of evil and especially the people who have lost their loved one and who lost their job. We have to stand together and move on with our lives, but not forget what happed. President Bush is going to make them pay for what they have done and I believe it will be soon.

I hope you
Feil Betr

Dear Rescue Workers,
Thank you for working very
late at night to save people.
You are heroes.

Children of all faiths and nationalities were affected by the events of September 11, as shown by the heart in a Star of David at right.

God Bless You all!

This letter is to whom ever lost someone in this tragedy.

If I could I would change everything> I know how it feels to lose someone because I lost my uncle in this incident. There's one thing I don't understand is why these people would do something like this. But what I do know is that these people will be punished for what they did. I feel that even though this tragedy has hurt alot of people "we all stand togeher."

I am Sorry for what Happend

I Love you

A simple "I love you" from a child has the ability to heal many hurts and griefs, and gives us hope for a better future.